INSPIRATION

365 Days A Year

By Zig Ziglar

Book Design: Vieceli Design Company, West Dundee, Illinois

Editing by Julie Kellogg

Photo Credits:

Nels Akerland—pages: 10, 18-19, 22, 27, 48, 60, 68-69, 80-81, 108-109, 132-133

Comstock, Julio Segura—pages: 2-3

Joe Decker—pages: 6-7, 40, 88, 152, 156-157

Jeff Vanuga—pages: 30-31, 34, 53, 72, 77, 94-95, 112, 117, 120-121, 136, 141

Bruce Heinemann—pages: 6-7, 98

Steve Terrill—pages: 36, 44-45, 56-57, 65, 84, 91, 102, 105, 124, 129, 144-145, 149

Introduction *by Zig Ziglar*

Reading has been the fuel of my motivation, it has changed the direction in which I have traveled, and it has enhanced my creative imagination more than any other activity I have ever pursued. I'm now in my eighth decade of living and I still read several hours a day. Why? When I can hook up old information with new information, the combination of the two creates perspectives that could never have been achieved otherwise. New information makes new and fresh ideas possible.

I read for the "ah-has," the information that makes a light bulb go off in my mind. **I want to put information in my mind that is going to be the most beneficial to me**, my family and my fellow man, financially, morally, spiritually, and emotionally. I seldom read anything that is not of a factual nature because I want to invest my time wisely in the things that will improve my life. Don't misunderstand; there is nothing wrong with reading purely for the joy of it. Novels have their place, but biographies of famous men and women contain information that can change lives. Dr. Norman Vincent Peale's, *The Power of Positive Thinking*, changed my thinking. The Bible changed my believing. Ultimately, what I have read has changed my being.

If the "ah-ha" I get when I'm reading is not already reduced into one or two sentences, I'll take the essence of what I've read and chunk it into easily remembered bites of information. That information is what becomes "quotable." You would not sit still for me to read every book I've ever read to you. But if you're the least bit like me, you'll jump at the chance to bypass all the churning and scoop the cream right off the top – that is what quotes are...the cream of our learning.

The right quote can inspire people to change their ways. I love to quote my mother, "Tell the truth and tell it ever, costeth what it will; for he who hides the wrong he did, does the wrong thing still." Of course this quote didn't begin with my mother, but she is the first person who said it to me. Quotes, good quotes, are like that – you remember who said it, what the circumstances were, and that it had an immediate impact on your thinking.

I've compiled the quotes in this book with great care. I've included quotes that will help you on the work front, the home front, and the spiritual front. There are quotes to lift you up and quotes to bring you back to earth. Some will make you smile and some will create more questions than you might care to think about. All of them will make you think and that is an exercise that will enhance and improve your future immensely.

It is my hope that you "get" the "ah-has" I got when I first read or wrote the quotes I've selected for this inspirational book.

If you apply what you learn to your life, I can honestly say that I will **See You at the Top!**

Zig Ziglar

JANUARY 1

Do what you can, with what you have, where you are.

— THEODORE ROOSEVELT

JANUARY 2

What lies behind us and what lies before us are tiny matters compared to what lies within us.

— RALPH WALDO EMERSON

JANUARY 3

In a time of drastic change it is the learners who inherit the future. The learned usually find themselves equipped to live in a world that no longer exists.

— ERIC HOFFER

JANUARY 4

Faith believes in spite of the circumstances and acts in spite of the consequences.

— ADRIAN ROGERS

JANUARY 5

Men are anxious to improve their circumstances, but are unwilling to improve themselves; they therefore remain bound.

— JAMES ALLEN, *As a Man Thinketh*

JANUARY 6

Life begins when you do.

— Hugh Downs

JANUARY 7

Anything worth doing is worth doing poorly — until you learn to do it well.

— Steve Brown

JANUARY 8

Great minds have purposes, others have wishes.

— Washington Irving

JANUARY 9

You can't be a smart cookie if you have a crummy attitude.

— John Maxwell

Great strength comes from within,
not from without.

— MARK BOWSER

JANUARY 11

We are free up to the point of **choice**; then the **choice controls the chooser**.

— MARY CROWLEY

JANUARY 12

Knowing thyself is the height of wisdom.

— SOCRATES

JANUARY 13

Most people who fail in their dreams fail not from lack of ability but from lack of commitment.

— ZIG ZIGLAR

When you have a **choice** and don't make it, that is in itself a choice.

— WILLIAM JAMES

God gives everyone certain attributes, characteristics, talents, and then He says, "If you use what you have I'll increase it, but if you don't use it, you'll lose it." Use it or lose it; it's a law.

— CHARLIE "TREMENDOUS" JONES

Action conquers fear.

— PETE ZARLENGA

JANUARY 17

Adversity is the first path to truth.

— George Gordon Byron

JANUARY 18

Don't be afraid to take a big step if needed. You can't cross a chasm in two small jumps.

— ANONYMOUS

JANUARY 19

Money is merely a reward for solving problems.

— Mike Murdock

JANUARY 20

The deepest principle in human nature is the craving to be appreciated.

— William James

Actions are seeds of fate. Seeds grow into destiny.

— Harry S. Truman

Eighty-five percent of the reason you get a job, keep that job, and move ahead in that job has to do with your people skills and people knowledge.

— Cavett Robert

Example is not the main thing in influencing others. It is the **only** thing.

— Albert Schweitzer

JANUARY 24

It is neither wealth nor splendor,
but tranquility and occupation,
which give happiness

Chop your own wood and it will warm you twice.

— Henry Ford

When you do the things you need to do when you need to do them, the day will come when you can do the things you want to do when you want to do them.

— Zig Ziglar

A loving person lives in a loving world. A hostile person lives in a hostile world. Everyone you meet is your mirror.

— Ken Keyes

JANUARY 28

Reputation is what others think about you; character is what God knows about you.

— Adrian Rogers

JANUARY 29

Input influences outlook, outlook influences output, and output determines outcome.

— Anonymous

JANUARY 30

All that we love deeply becomes a part of us.

— Helen Keller

JANUARY 31

Each of us will one day be judged by our standard of life, not by our standard of living; by our measure of giving, not by our measure of wealth; by our simple goodness, not by our seeming greatness.

— William Arthur Ward

FEBRUARY 1

A vision is a clearly-articulated, results-oriented picture of a future you intend to create. It is a dream with direction.

— Jesse Stoner Zemel

FEBRUARY 2

Until you commit your goals to paper, you have intentions that are seeds without soil.

— Anonymous

FEBRUARY 3

It's the little things that make the big things possible. Only close attention to the fine details of any operation makes the operation first class.

— J. Willard Marriott

FEBRUARY 4

If you aren't fired with enthusiasm, you will be fired with enthusiasm.

— Vince Lombardi

FEBRUARY 5

People spend their lives in the service of their passions instead of employing their passions in the service of their lives.

— Sir Richard Steele

FEBRUARY 6

People will not bear it when advice is violently given, even if it is well founded. Hearts are flowers; they remain open to the softly falling dew, but shut up in the violent downpour of rain.

— JOHN PAUL RICHTER

FEBRUARY 7

Evidence is conclusive that your self-talk has a direct bearing on your performance.

— ZIG ZIGLAR

FEBRUARY 8

Wealth is not measured by just what we have, but rather by what we have for which we would not take money.

— ANONYMOUS

FEBRUARY 9

It's in the struggle itself that you define yourself.

— PAT BUCHANAN

FEBRUARY 10

Time flies. It's up to you
to be the **navigator**.

— Robert Orben

FEBRUARY 11

Gratitude conserves the vital energies of a person more than any other attitude tested.
— Hans Selye

FEBRUARY 12

A good marriage is when you're married not to someone you can live with, but to someone you really cannot live without.

— Dr. Howard Hendricks

Choice, not chance, determines human destiny.

— ROBERT W. ELLIS

No one can make you feel inferior without your consent.

— ELEANOR ROOSEVELT

FEBRUARY 15

Only those who constantly retool themselves stand a chance of staying employed in the years ahead.

— Tom Peters

FEBRUARY 16

It's not what you know or who you know. It's what you are that finally counts.

— Zig Ziglar

FEBRUARY 17

Until you make peace with who you are you will never be content with what you have.

— Doris Mortman

FEBRUARY 18

It's not your position in life; it's the disposition you have which will change your position.

— Dr. David McKinley

FEBRUARY 19

The core problem is not that we are too passionate about bad things, but that we are not passionate enough about good things.

— Larry Crabb

FEBRUARY 20

In the middle of every difficulty comes opportunity.

— Albert Einstein

FEBRUARY 21

The happiness of most people we know is not ruined by great catastrophes or fatal errors, but by the repetition of slowly destructive little things.

— Ernest Dimnet

FEBRUARY 22

It's not where you start — it's where you finish that counts.

—Zig Ziglar

Skill to do comes of doing.

— Ralph Waldo Emerson

Seek to do good and you will find that happiness will run after you.

— James Freeman Clarke

If a person doesn't govern his temper, his temper will govern him.

— John Maxwell

FEBRUARY 26

There is only one way to succeed at anything and that is to give everything.

— Vince Lombardi

FEBRUARY 27

Think big thoughts, but relish small pleasures.

— H. Jackson Brown

FEBRUARY 28

If what you believe doesn't affect how you live, then it isn't very important.

— Dick Nogleberg

MARCH 1

As I grow older part of my emotional survival plan must be to actively seek inspiration instead of passively waiting for it to find me.

— BEBE MOORE CAMPBELL

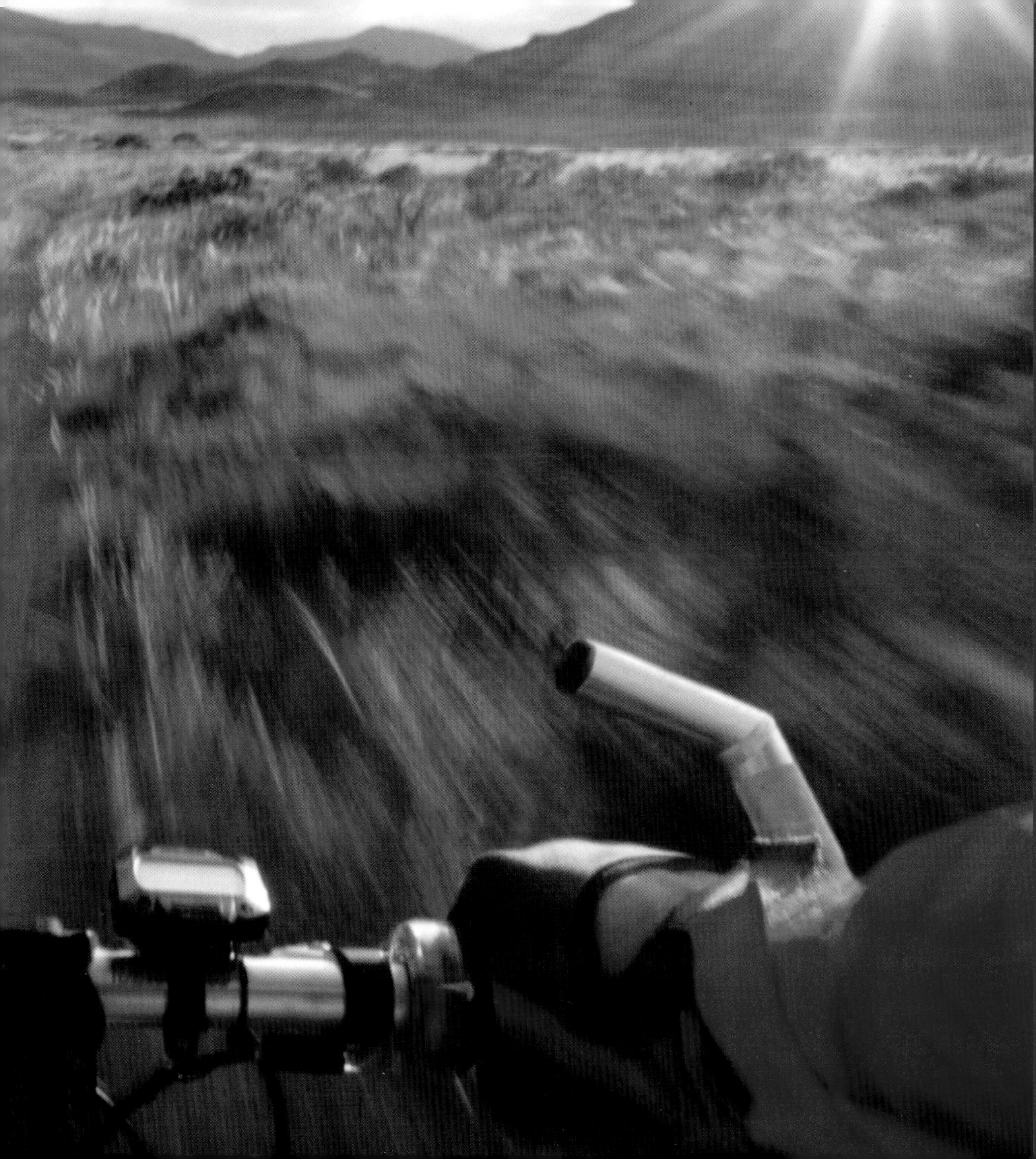

MARCH 2

You will become as small as your controlling desire;
as great as your dominant aspiration.

— James Allen

MARCH 3

The world is but a canvas to the imagination.

— Henry David Thoreau

MARCH 4

Remember, happiness doesn't depend on who you are or what
you have; it depends solely upon what you think.

— Dale Carnegie

MARCH 5

The only thing we have to fear is fear itself.

— Franklin Delano Roosevelt

MARCH 6

The most important thing about goals is… having one.

— GEOFFRY F. ABERT

MARCH 7

Who has not served cannot command.

— JOHN FLORIO

MARCH 8

Success Procedure: Run your day by the clock and your life with a vision.

— ZIG ZIGLAR

We have a right to choose our attitude.

— Viktor Frankl

I am always talking about the human condition, about what we can endure, dream, fail at and still survive.

— Maya Angelou

You are the way you are because that's the way you want to be. If you really wanted to be any different, you would be in the process of changing right now.

— Fred Smith

MARCH 12

Even if you're on the right track, you'll get run over if you just sit there.

— Will Rogers

MARCH 13

In your hands you hold the **seeds of failure or the potential for greatness.** Your hands are capable, but they must be used and for the right things to reap the rewards you are capable of attaining. The choice is yours.

— Zig Ziglar

MARCH 14

The supreme accomplishment is to blur the line between work and play.

— Arnold Toynbee

MARCH 15

Graciousness is more than good manners. It is more than courtesy. It is the etiquette of the soul. True graciousness has such a divine quality we feel it is something that comes through us and not from us.

— Fred Smith

MARCH 16

The only difference between successful people and unsuccessful people is extraordinary determination.

— Mary Kay Ash

MARCH 17

If one advances confidently in the direction of his dreams and endeavors to live the life which he has imagined, he will meet with a success unexpected in common hours. If you have built castles in the air, your work need not be lost. That is where they should be. Now put the foundations under them.

— HENRY DAVID THOREAU

MARCH 18

Self-respect is the fruit of discipline.

— ABRAHAM J. HESCHEL

MARCH 19

The most important thing is your self-respect. It doesn't matter what people think about you, but what you think about yourself.

— ROBERT H. ABPLANALP

MARCH 20

Every crucial experience can be regarded as a setback — or the start of a new kind of development.

— MARY ROBERTS KINEHART

MARCH 21

You can't wait for inspiration. You have to go after it with a club.

— JACK LONDON

MARCH 22

I am grateful for all of my problems. After each one was overcome, I became stronger and more able to meet those that were still to come. I grew in all my difficulties.

— J. C. PENNEY

MARCH 23

You can't talk yourself out of a problem you behave yourself into. — STEPHEN COVEY

MARCH 24

Success is the sum of small efforts – repeated day in and day out.

— ROBERT COLLIER

When you believe and think **"I can,"** you activate your motivation, commitment, confidence, concentration and excitement – all of which relate directly to achievement. — Dr. Jerry Lynch

If you would lift me up you must be on higher ground.

— Ralph Waldo Emerson

There is no such thing as a minor lapse of integrity.

— Tom Peters

MARCH 28

Success comes from taking the hand you were dealt and using it to the very best of your ability.

— Ty Boyd

MARCH 29

We must become the change we wish to see in the world.

— Mahatma Gandhi

MARCH 30

You know you are old when you have lost all your marvels.

— Merry Browne

MARCH 31

Defeat should never be a source of discouragement, but rather a fresh stimulus.

— Robert South

APRIL 1

Your greatness is measured
by your horizons.

— Michelangelo

Experience shows that success is due less to ability than to zeal. The winner is he who gives himself to his work, body and soul.

— CHARLES BEXTON

Enjoyment is not a goal. It is a feeling that accompanies important, on-going activity.

— PAUL GOODMAN

Failure should be our teacher, not our undertaker. Failure is delay, not defeat. It is a temporary detour, not a dead end.

— DENIS WAITLEY

APRIL 5

Discipline is the habit of taking consistent action until one can perform with unconscious competence. Discipline weighs ounces but regret weighs tons.

— JHOON RHEE

APRIL 6

Four short words sum up what lifted most successful individuals above the crowd: **a little bit more**. They did all that was expected of them and…a little bit more.

— A. LOU VICKERY

APRIL 7

If you want to get the best out of a person you must look for the best that is in him.

— BERNARD HALDANE

APRIL 8

Three billion people on the face of the earth go to bed hungry every night, but four billion people go to bed every night hungry for a simple word of encouragement and recognition.

— CAVETT ROBERT

APRIL 9

The biggest tragedy in America is not the great waste of natural resources – though this is tragic; the biggest tragedy is the waste of human resources because the average person goes to his grave with his music still in him.

— OLIVER WENDELL HOLMES

APRIL 10

Optimism is the faith that leads to achievement. Nothing can be done without hope and confidence.

— HELEN KELLER

APRIL 11

True grit is making a decision and standing by it, doing what must be done.

— JOHN WAYNE

APRIL 12

Ninety percent of all those who fail are not actually defeated. They simply quit.

— Paul J. Meyer

APRIL 13

If you learn only methods, you'll be tied to your methods. But if you learn principles, you can devise your own methods.

— Ralph Waldo Emerson

APRIL 14

How far you go in life depends on your being tender with the young, compassionate with the aged, sympathetic with the striving, and tolerant of the weak and the strong. Because someday in life you will have been all of these.

— George Washington Carver

APRIL 15

A person is not defeated by their opponents but by themselves.

— Jan Christiaan Smuts

A person can succeed at almost anything for which they have unlimited enthusiasm.

— Charles M. Schwab

APRIL 17

No matter how bad someone has it, there are others who have it worse. Remembering that makes life a lot easier and allows you to take pleasure in the blessings you have been given.

— Lou Holtz

APRIL 18

Common sense is genius dressed up in work clothes.

— Ralph Waldo Emerson

APRIL 19

Genius is 1% inspiration and 99% perspiration.

— Thomas A. Edison

Ability without honor has no value.

— Ralph Waldo Emerson

APRIL 21

Do a little more than you're paid to. Give a little more than you have to. Try a little harder than you want to. Aim a little higher than you think possible, and give a lot of thanks to God for health, family and friends.

— Art Linkletter

APRIL 22

The fear of rejection or failure creates inaction.

— John Maxwell

APRIL 23

Hope never dies where faith is strong, and faith grows strong in the presence of hope.

— Chad Witmeyer

APRIL 24

Faith is taking the first step even when you don't see the whole staircase.

The message is clear:
Plan with attitude,
prepare with aptitude,
participate with servitude,
receive with gratitude, and
this should be enough to
separate you from the
multitudes.

— KRISH DHANAM

Character is what you are in the dark.

— D. L. MOODY

APRIL 27

Passion, for all its dangers, needs uncaging if we are to move towards completeness as human beings.

— PHILIP SHELDRAKE

APRIL 28

Real optimism is aware of problems but recognizes solutions; knows about difficulties but believes they can be overcome; sees the negatives, but accentuates the positives; is exposed to the worst but expects the best; has reason to complain, but chooses to smile.

— WILLIAM ARTHUR WARD

APRIL 29

Blind zeal is soon put to a shameful retreat, while holy resolution, built on fast principles, lifts up its head like a rock in the midst of the waves.

— WILLIAM GURNALL

APRIL 30

I never think of the future. It comes soon enough.

— ALBERT EINSTEIN

MAY 1

The doors of wisdom are never shut.

— BEN FRANKLIN

An optimist is someone who believes that a house fly is looking for a way to get out.

— GEORGE GENE NATHAN

Character is not in the mind; it is in the will.

— FULTON J. SHEEN

The most important opinion is the one you have of yourself, and the most significant things you say all day are those things you say to yourself.

— ZIG ZIGLAR

MAY 5

When your goals are clearly defined and intelligently set, you have, in essence, taken a major step toward programming your left brain. That frees your right brain to be its creative best.

— Zig Ziglar

MAY 6

We make a living by what we get, but we make a life by what we give.

— Winston Churchill

MAY 7

The world is moving so fast these days that the person who says it can't be done is generally interrupted by someone doing it.

— Elbert Hubbard

MAY 8

The work of the individual still remains the spark that moves mankind forward.

— Igor Sikorsky

Only passions, **great passions,** can
elevate the soul to great things.

— DENIS DIDEROT

MAY 10

Your neighbors will make judgments about you based on how your lawn
and house look, and people who see you in passing will judge you based on
how clean you keep your car. It's not always fair, but it has always been true.
Appearances matter, so make yours a good one.

— Lou Holtz

MAY 11

Success on any major scale requires you to accept
responsibility. In the final analysis, the one quality
that all successful people have is the ability to take
on responsibility.

— Michael Korda

MAY 12

**Marriages may be made in Heaven but a lot of the
details have to be worked out here on Earth.**

— Gloria Pitzer

MAY 13

Blessed are those who dream dreams and are willing to
pay the price to make them come true.

— Henry Viscardi, Jr.

Passion is born the moment you catch a glimpse of your potential.

— FRED SMITH

A winner is big enough to admit his mistakes, smart enough to profit from them, and strong enough to correct them.

— JOHN MAXWELL

Success means having the courage, the determination, and the will to become the person you believe you were meant to be.

— GEORGE SHEEHAN

MAY 17

The way you see your future determines your thinking today. Your thinking today determines your performance today. Your performance in the todays of your life determines your future.

— Zig Ziglar

MAY 18

A true commitment is a heart-felt promise to yourself from which you will not back down.

— David McNally

MAY 19

A sense of humor snuffs out our sparks of friction before they get to our fuel tank.

— Fred Smith

Most Americans honestly believe America is the most powerful nation on earth, but actually the most powerful nation is **imagi**-nation.

— Zig Ziglar

When dads shoot straight, the kids will hit the mark.

— Adrian Rogers

We shall never know all the good that a simple smile can do.

— Mother Teresa

MAY 23

Our words reveal our thoughts; manners mirror our self-esteem; our actions reflect our character; our habits predict the future.

— WILLIAM ARTHUR WARD

MAY 24

Love is life…and if you miss love, you miss life.

— Leo Buscaglia

MAY 25

It's one of the most beautiful compensations of this life that no man can sincerely try to help another without helping himself.

— Ralph Waldo Emerson

MAY 26

If you judge people, you don't have time to love them.

— Mother Teresa

MAY 27

God never consults your past to determine your future.

— Mike Murdock

MAY 28

Nothing in this world can take the place of persistence. Talent will not; Nothing is more common than unsuccessful people with talent. Genius will not; Unrewarded genius is almost a proverb. Education will not; the world is full of educated derelicts. Persistence and determination alone are omnipotent.

— Calvin Coolidge

MAY 29

You're never a loser until you quit trying.

— Mike Ditka

MAY 30

There is no doubt in my mind that there are many ways to be a winner, but there is only one way to be a loser and that is to fail and not look beyond that failure.

— Kyle Rote, Jr.

MAY 31

If you have a great ambition, take as big a step as possible in the direction of fulfilling it, but if the step is only a tiny one, don't worry if it is the largest one now possible.

— Mildred McAfee

Narrow-minded people are similar to narrow-necked bottles. The less they have in them the more noise they make pouring it out.

— ALEXANDER POPE

JUNE 2

Many things will catch your eye, but only a few will catch your heart...pursue those.

— ANONYMOUS

JUNE 3

What counts is not necessarily the size of the dog in the fight — it's the size of the fight in the dog.

— DWIGHT D. EISENHOWER

JUNE 4

The best way out is always through.

— ROBERT FROST

JUNE 5

The U. S. Constitution doesn't guarantee happiness, only the pursuit of it. You have to catch up with it yourself.

—BENJAMIN FRANKLIN

JUNE 6

Success is not measured by what a person accomplishes, but by the opposition they have encountered, and the courage with which they have maintained the struggle against overwhelming odds.

— Orison Swett Marden

JUNE 7

You don't have to be great to start, but you have to start to be great.

— Joe Sabah

JUNE 8

Kids don't make up 100% of our population, but they do make up 100% of our future.

— Zig Ziglar

JUNE 9

There are two ways of spreading light:
to be the candle or the mirror that reflects it.

— EDITH WHARTON

JUNE 10

Friendship is the only cement that will ever hold the world together.

— WOODROW WILSON

JUNE 11

Happiness is a conscious choice, not an automatic response.

— MILDRED BARTHEL

JUNE 12

Not in the clamor of the crowded street, nor in the shouts and plaudits of the throng, but in ourselves are triumph and defeat.

— HENRY WADSWORTH LONGFELLOW

A happy person is not a person in a certain set of circumstances, but rather a person with a certain set of attitudes.

— Hugh Downs

The difference between success and failure is often about 5% more effort.

— S. Truett Cathy

We can't choose our relatives, but we can choose our thoughts – which influence us much more.

— Anonymous

JUNE 16

Failure is an event, not a person. So regardless of what happens to you along the way, you must keep on going and doing the right thing in the right way. Then the event becomes a reality of a changed life.

— Zig Ziglar

JUNE 17

Do not wish to be anything but what you are, and try to be that perfectly.

— St. Francis de Sales

JUNE 18

I learned a great many new words that day. I do not remember what they all were, but I do know that mother, father, sister, teacher were among them – words that were to make the world blossom for me "like Aaron's rod, with flowers." It would have been difficult to find a happier child than I was as I lay in my bed at the close of that eventful day and lived over the joys it had brought me, and for the first time longed for a new day to come.

— Helen Keller

If you are wearing out the seat of your pants before you do your shoe soles, you are making too many contacts in the wrong place.

— Anonymous

It is better to be divided by truth than to be united by error.

— Adrian Rogers

I read myself out of poverty long before I worked myself out of poverty.

— Walter Anderson

Happiness is not in our circumstances but in ourselves. It is not something we see, like a rainbow, or feel, like the heat of a fire. Happiness is something we are.

— John D. Sheerin

JUNE 23

Regardless of your lot in life, you can build something beautiful on it.

— Zig Ziglar

JUNE 24

Motivation is the spark that lights the fire of knowledge and fuels the engine of accomplishment. It maximizes and maintains momentum.

— Zig Ziglar

JUNE 25

Some people think they have burning ambition when it is merely inflammation of the wishbone.

— *Cross Roads*, the book

JUNE 26

Each day comes bearing its own gifts. Untie the ribbons.

— Ruth Ann Schabacker

JUNE 27

Men and women are limited not by the place of their birth, not by the color of their skin, but by the size of their hope.

— John Johnson

JUNE 28

By nature we have no defect that could not become a strength, no strength that could not become a defect.

— Johann Wolfgang von Goethe

JUNE 29

It's always better to face the truth, no matter how uncomfortable, than to continue coddling a lie.

— Lou Holtz

JUNE 30

Nothing great was ever achieved without enthusiasm.

— Ralph Waldo Emerson

Decision is the spark that ignites action. Until a decision is made nothing happens. — Wilfred A. Peterson

It is easy to dodge our responsibilities, but we cannot dodge the consequences of dodging our responsibilities.

— Sir Josiah Stamp

The greatest good we can do for anyone is not to share our wealth with them, but rather to reveal their own wealth to them. It's astonishing how much talent and ability rests inside a human being.

— Zig Ziglar

JULY 4

Too often the opportunity knocks, but by the time you disengage the chain, push back the bolt, unhook the two locks and shut off the burglar alarms, it's too late.

— RITA COOLIDGE

JULY 5

Some people drink at the fountain of knowledge. Others just gargle.

— ANONYMOUS

JULY 6

How much more grievous are the consequences of anger than the causes of it?

— MARCUS AURELIUS

JULY 7

Reading makes a man full.

— FRANCIS BACON

JULY 8

The highest point of achievement yesterday is the starting point of today.

— MOTTO OF PAULIST FATHERS

JULY 9

When you clearly understand that success is a process, not an event, you are encouraged to follow the right process to create the success you are capable of having.

— Zig Ziglar

JULY 10

An investment in knowledge pays the best interest.

— Ben Franklin

JULY 11

You can make your life whatever you want it to be.

— Wally Amos

JULY 12

Training teaches people what to do; education teaches people what to be.

— Nido R. Qubein

JULY 13

A great leader's courage to fulfill his vision comes from passion, not position.

— John Maxwell

JULY 14

Your past is important because it brought you to where you are, but as important as your past is, it is not nearly as important as the way you see your future.

— Dr. Tony Campolo

JULY 15

If you have a tendency to brag just remember it's not the whistle that pulls the train.

— O. F. Nichols

JULY 16

It's not what happens to me, it's what happens in me. It's not the size of the problem, but how I handle the problem when I fall.

— Greg Horn

JULY 17

Quality is never an accident. It is always the result of intelligent effort.

— John Ruskin

JULY 18

Grandmother/grandchild relationships are simple: Grandmas are short on criticism and long on love.

— Anonymous

JULY 19

Happiness is not a when or a where; it can be a here and a now. But until you are happy with who you are you will never be happy because of what you have.

— Zig Ziglar

JULY 20

Weakness of attitude becomes weakness of character.

— ALBERT EINSTEIN

JULY 21

Every production of genius must be the production of enthusiasm.

— BENJAMIN DISRAELI

JULY 22

The greatest use we can make of our life is to spend it on something that outlasts it.

— *CROSS ROADS*, THE BOOK

JULY 23

What a bargain grandchildren are! I give them my loose change and they give me a million dollars' worth of pleasure.

— GENE PERRET

JULY 24

Children have never been very good at listening to their elders, but they've never failed to imitate them.

— James Baldwin

You might not be what you say you are, but what you say, you are.

— ZIG ZIGLAR

He climbs highest who helps another up.

— GEORGE MATTHEW ADAMS

Husbands, if you treat your wife like a thoroughbred, chances are good you won't end up with a nag. Wives, if you treat your husband like a champ, chances are even better that you won't end up with a chump.

— ZIG ZIGLAR

All we need to make us really happy is something to be enthusiastic about.

— CHARLES KINGSLEY

JULY 29

A journey of a thousand miles begins with a single step.

— Chinese Proverb

JULY 30

Adversity causes some people to break; others to break records.

— William A. Ward

JULY 31

If there is to be any peace, it will come through being – not having.

— Henry Miller

AUGUST 1

Mountaintops inspire leaders
but valleys mature them.

— J. Philip Everson

Recognizing a problem or weakness is the first step in remedying it.

— Donald Laird

Watch your thoughts, **they become** words.
Watch your words, **they become** actions.
Watch your actions, **they become** habits.
Watch your habits, **they become** character.
Watch your character, **it becomes your** destiny.

— Frank Outlaw

Be open, obvious, and a sincere listener.
Denial is not just a river in Egypt; denial is
ignoring the obvious.

— Dr. Stephen Covey

Well done is better than well said.

— BEN FRANKLIN

Though no one can go back and make a brand new start, anyone can start from now and make a brand new ending.

— CARL BARD

A problem is something that can be solved. A fact of life is something that must be accepted.

—JOHN MAXWELL

The truth is, fear and immorality are two of the greatest inhibitors of performance.

— ZIG ZIGLAR

AUGUST 9

Pleasure is very seldom found where it is sought. Our brightest blazes are commonly kindled by unexpected sparks.

— SAMUEL JOHNSON

AUGUST 10

The price of greatness is responsibility.

— WINSTON CHURCHILL

AUGUST 11

The history of free men is never really written by chance but by choice, their choice!

— DWIGHT D. EISENHOWER

AUGUST 12

It is not the brains that matter most, but that which guides them: the character, the heart, generous qualities, progressive ideas.

— FYODOR DOSTOYEVSKY

When I was young I observed that nine out of every ten things I did were failures, so I did ten times more work.

— George Bernard Shaw

When the going gets tough, those with a dream keep going.

— Ben Feldman

In our country you are free to choose but the choices you make today will determine what you will be, do and have in the tomorrows of your life.

— Zig Ziglar

AUGUST 16

There is an advantage in every disadvantage, and a gift in every problem.

— John Johnson

AUGUST 17

A pleasing personality helps you win friends and influence people. Add character to that formula and you keep those friends and maintain the influence.

— Zig Ziglar

AUGUST 18

The difference between greatness and mediocrity is often how an individual views a mistake.

— Nelson Boswell

AUGUST 19

Grandchildren are God's way of compensating us for growing old.

— Mary H. Waldrip

AUGUST 20

What you get by achieving your goals is not as important as what you become by achieving your goals.

— Zig Ziglar

Caring about others, running the risk of feeling and leaving an impact on people, brings happiness.

— RABBI HAROLD KUSHNER

A person hears only what they understand.

— JOHANN WOLFGANG VON GOETHE

A strong passion for any object will ensure success, for the desire of the end will point out the means.

— WILLIAM HAZLITT

AUGUST 24

Every problem has in it the seeds of its own solution.
If you don't have any problems, you don't get any seeds.

— NORMAN VINCENT PEALE

You can have total success when you balance your physical, mental and spiritual, as well as your personal, family and business life.

— Zig Ziglar

Civilizations do not give out; they give in. In a society where anything goes, eventually everything will.

— John Underwood

Procrastination is opportunity's natural assassin.

— Victor Kiam

Security comes from your ability to produce. In short, it is an inside job.

—General Douglas MacArthur

AUGUST 29

Much of what we see depends
on what we are looking for.

— Phil Callloway

AUGUST 30

We can do no great things – only small things with great love.

— Mother Teresa

AUGUST 31

We all find time to do what we really want to do.

— William Feather

People were designed for accomplishment, engineered for success, and endowed with the seeds of greatness.

— Zig Ziglar

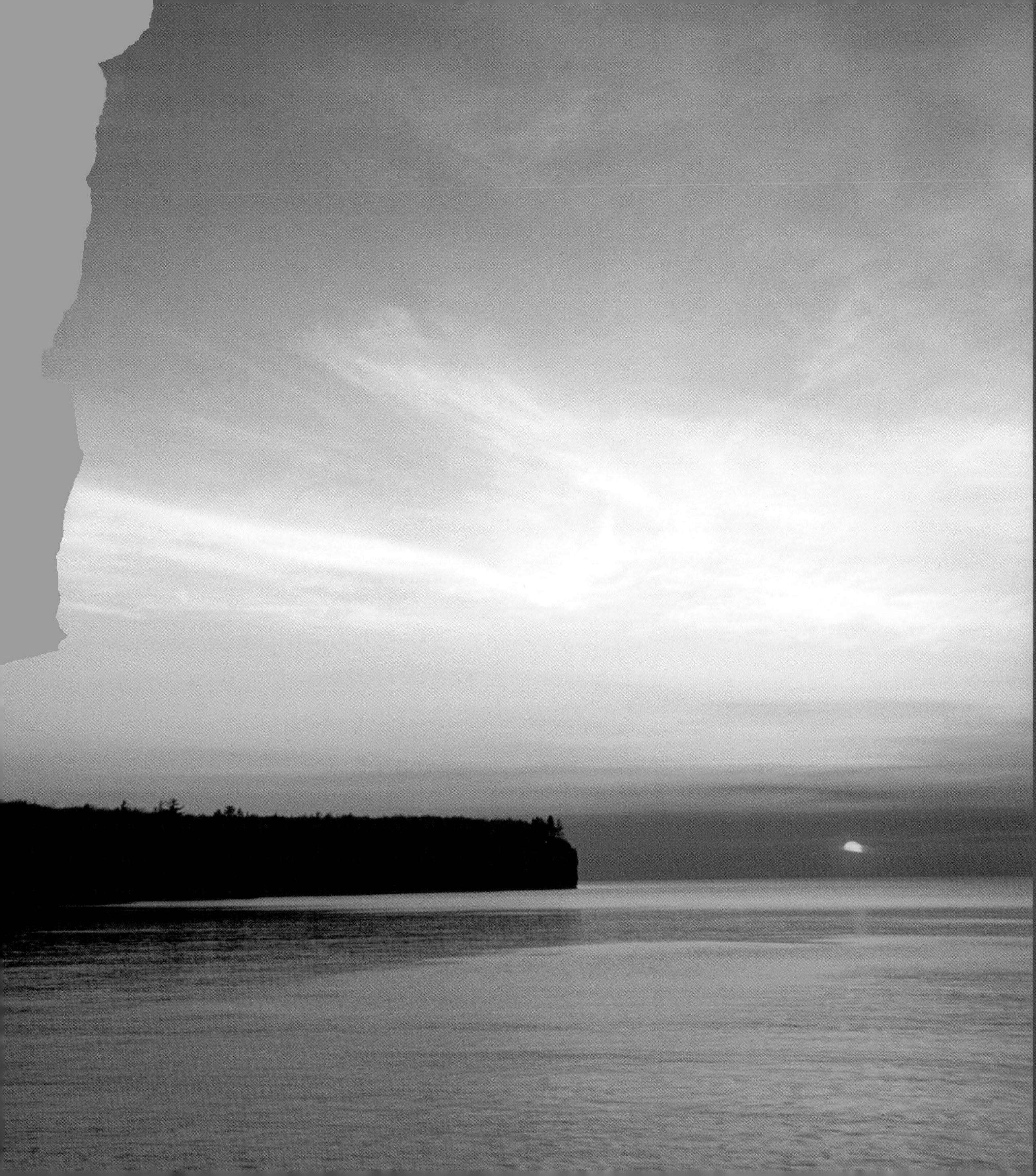

SEPTEMBER 2

True discipline isn't on your back,
needling you with imperatives. It is at
your side, nudging you with incentives.

— SYBIL STANTON

SEPTEMBER 3

When there is no hope in the future there is no power in the present.

— JOHN MAXWELL

SEPTEMBER 4

What a man knows only through feeling
can be explained only through enthusiasm.

— JOSEPH JOUBERT

SEPTEMBER 5

You can have everything in life you want if you will just help enough other people get what they want.

— Zig Ziglar

SEPTEMBER 6

One learns people through the heart, not the eyes or the intellect.

— Mark Twain

SEPTEMBER 7

You win a few, you lose a few. Some get rained out. But you got to dress for all of them.

— Leroy Satchel Paige

SEPTEMBER 8

Without hope, people are only half alive. With hope they dream and think and work.

— Charles Sawyer

If you don't think every day is a good day,
just try missing one.

— CAVETT ROBERT

SEPTEMBER 10

Character is the total of thousands of small daily strivings to live up to the best that is in us.

— Lt. Gen. Arthur Trudeau

SEPTEMBER 11

The secret of happiness is to admire without desiring.

— F. H. Bradley

SEPTEMBER 12

We deny our talents and abilities because to acknowledge or to confess them would commit us to use them.

— Zig Ziglar

SEPTEMBER 13

You can't have rosy thoughts about the future when your mind is full of blues about the past.

— Tidbits

A goal casually set and lightly taken is freely abandoned at the first obstacle.

— ZIG ZIGLAR

Progress involves risks. You can't steal second base and keep your foot on first.

— FREDERICK B. WILCOX

When patterns are broken, new worlds emerge.

— TULI KUPFERBERG

Refusal to hope is nothing more than a decision to die.

— BERNIE S. SIEGEL, M.D.

SEPTEMBER 18

Opportunity may knock once, but temptation bangs on your front door forever.

— Anonymous

SEPTEMBER 19

There aren't nearly enough crutches in the world for all the lame excuses.

— Marcus Stroup

SEPTEMBER 20

Obstacles are those frightful things you see when you take your eyes off your goals.

— Sydney Smith

A compliment is the lift in the elevator of life.

— Sue Cox

A vision without a task is but a dream. A task without a vision is drudgery. A vision and a task are the hope of the world.

— Quote on a church wall in Sussex, England

Eyes that look are common; eyes that see are rare.

— J. Oswald Sanders

SEPTEMBER 24

Learning is not compulsory...neither is survival.

— W. Edwards Deming

Our business in life is not to get ahead of others, but to get ahead of ourselves, to break our own records, to outstrip our yesterday by our today.

— STUART B. JOHNSON

Never lose sight of the fact that the most important yardstick of your success will be how you treat other people.

— BARBARA BUSH

SEPTEMBER 27

The larger the island of knowledge, the longer the shoreline of wonder.

— RALPH W. STOCKMAN

SEPTEMBER 28

I have never met an unhappy giver.

— GEORGE ADAMS

SEPTEMBER 29

You can't change the past, but you can ruin a perfectly good present by worrying about the future.

— ANONYMOUS

SEPTEMBER 30

Life is not about waiting for the storms to pass...it's about learning how to dance in the rain.

— ANONYMOUS

You have been given citizenship in a country like none other on earth, with opportunities available to you like nowhere else on earth. What will be asked of you is hard work; nothing will be handed to you.... Use your education and success in life to help those still trapped in cycles of poverty and violence. Above all, never lose faith in America. Its faults are yours to fix, not to curse.

— GENERAL COLIN POWELL

OCTOBER 2

The bee is more honored than other animals, not because she labors, but because she labors for others.

— St. John Chrysostom

OCTOBER 3

There is a time to let things happen and a time to make things happen.

— Hugh Prather

OCTOBER 4

What I hear I forget. What I see I remember. What I do, I know.

— Chinese Proverb

OCTOBER 5

The mediocre teacher tells; the good teacher explains; the superior teacher demonstrates; the great teacher inspires.

— William Arthur Ward

OCTOBER 6

I can't sit back and fold my hands and think about the past, for there are thousands of yesterdays but only one today and...maybe a tomorrow.

— Red Skelton

OCTOBER 7

Opportunities are seldom labeled.

— Claude McDonald

OCTOBER 8

If you could get up the courage to begin, you have the courage to succeed.

— David Viscott

OCTOBER 9

Wisdom is knowledge which has become a part of one's being.

— Orrison Swett Marden

OCTOBER 10

He that cannot forgive others breaks the bridge over which he, himself, must pass.

—Lord Herbert

OCTOBER 11

I bring you the gift of these four words: I believe in you.

— Blaise Pascal

OCTOBER 12

Success is often nothing more than moving from one failure to the next with undiminished enthusiasm.

— Winston Churchill

OCTOBER 13

The longer we follow the right path the easier it becomes.

— Anonymous

A good leader takes more than their fair share of the blame and gives more than their share of the credit.

— Arnold Glasnow

Man's mind, once stretched by a new idea, never regains its original dimensions.

— Oliver Wendell Holmes

Win without boasting. Lose without excuses.

— Vince Lombardi

OCTOBER 17

The real voyage of discovery consists not in seeking new landscapes but in having new eyes.

— MARCEL PROUST

OCTOBER 18

If one advances confidently in the direction of their dreams, and endeavors to live the life they've imagined, they will meet success unexpected in common hours.

— HENRY DAVID THOREAU

OCTOBER 19

Failure is the opportunity to begin again, this time more intelligently.

— HENRY FORD

OCTOBER 20

Your aspirations are your possibilities.

— SAMUEL JOHNSON

OCTOBER 21

The quality of a person's life is in direct proportion to their commitment to excellence, regardless of their chosen field of endeavor.

— VINCE LOMBARDI

OCTOBER 22

Failure is success if we learn from it.

— MALCOLM FORBES

OCTOBER 23

Success is focusing the full power of all you are on what you have a burning desire to achieve.

— WINFRED PETERSON

OCTOBER 24

Faith is knowing there is an ocean because you have seen a brook.

— WILLIAM ARTHUR WARD

129

A well-developed sense of humor is the pole that adds balance to your steps as you walk the tightrope of life.

— WILLIAM A. WARD

A stumble may prevent a fall.

— THOMAS FULLER

If passion drives you, let reason hold the reins.

— BENJAMIN FRANKLIN

OCTOBER 28

Sometimes we all need to realize that negative thoughts have no power. We empower them.

— Kurt Goad

OCTOBER 29

A single idea can transform a person, a life, a business, a nation, a world.

— Anonymous

OCTOBER 30

Chance favors the prepared mind.

— Louis Pasteur

OCTOBER 31

Success seems to be connected with action. Successful people keep moving. They make mistakes, but they don't quit.

— Conrad Hilton

NOVEMBER 1

I found that the men and women who got to the top were those that did the jobs they had in hand with everything they had of energy, enthusiasm and hard work.

— HARRY TRUMAN

People are like sticks of dynamite. The power's on the inside but nothing happens until the fuse gets lit.

— MAC ANDERSON

Some men see things as they are and say "why?" I dream things that never were, and say "why not?"

— GEORGE BERNARD SHAW

The difference between failure and success is doing a thing nearly right and doing it exactly right.

— ANONYMOUS

Consider every mistake you do make as an asset.

— PAUL J. MEYER

NOVEMBER 6

It is a funny thing about life; if you refuse to accept anything but the best you very often get it.

— W. Somerset Maugham

NOVEMBER 7

Happiness is a choice, not a response.

—Anonymous

NOVEMBER 8

This one step – choosing a goal and sticking to it – changes everything.

— Scott Reed

NOVEMBER 9

They who would accomplish little must sacrifice little; they who would achieve much must sacrifice much.

— James Allen

NOVEMBER 10

You may have to fight a battle more than once to win it.

— Margaret Thatcher

NOVEMBER 11

Give the world the best you have and the best will come back to you.

— MADELINE BRIDGES

NOVEMBER 12

He who sows courtesy reaps friendship, and he who plants kindness gathers love.

— SAINT BASIL

It is impossible to win the race unless you venture to run, impossible to win the victory unless you dare to battle.

— Richard M. DeVos

The miracle, or the power, that elevates the few is to be found in their industry, application, and perseverance under the prompting of a brave, determined spirit.

— Mark Twain

The service we render others is the rent we pay for our room on earth.

— Wilfred Grenfell

NOVEMBER 16

No matter how much time you've wasted in the past, you still have all of tomorrow. Success depends upon using it wisely by planning and setting priorities. The fact is, time is worth more than money, and by killing time we are killing our own chances for success.

— DENIS WAITLEY

NOVEMBER 17

Great works are performed not by strength but by perseverance.

— SAMUEL JOHNSON

NOVEMBER 18

The heart that gives...gathers.

— HANNAH MOORE

NOVEMBER 19

Make the most of yourself, for that is all there is of you.

— RALPH WALDO EMERSON

NOVEMBER 20

We are what and where we are because we have first imagined it.

— DONALD CURTIS

NOVEMBER 21

Anyone can hold the helm when the sea is calm.

— PUBLILIUS SYRUS

NOVEMBER 22

To love what you do and feel that it matters – how could anything be more fun?

— KATHARINE GRAHAM

NOVEMBER 23

A quiet conscience sleeps in thunder.

— ENGLISH PROVERB

You seldom come across anything more enjoyable than a happy person.

— FRANK A. CLARK

It is not the things we get, but the hearts we touch, that will measure our success in life.

— ANONYMOUS

It's the constant and determined effort that breaks down all resistance, sweeps away all obstacles.

— CLAUDE M. BRISTOL

NOVEMBER 27

Life is like a game of tennis; the player who serves well seldom loses.

— Anonymous

NOVEMBER 28

The people who get on in this world are the people who get up and look for the circumstances they want, and, if they can't find them, make them.

— George Bernard Shaw

NOVEMBER 29

Money never made anyone rich.

— Seneca

NOVEMBER 30

Much of what we see depends on what we are looking for.

— Phil Calloway

DECEMBER 1

No one is useless in this world who lightens
the burden of it to anyone else.

— CHARLES DICKENS

Commitment is what transforms a promise to reality.

— ANONYMOUS

The life of a winner is the result of an unswerving commitment to a never-ending process of self-completion.

— TERRY BRADSHAW

Courage is resistance to fear, mastery of fear — not absence of fear.

— MARK TWAIN

Our ego is our silent partner – too often with a controlling interest.

— CULLEN HIGHTOWER

DECEMBER 6

Anger is the wind that blows out the lamp of the mind.

— ROBERT G. INGERSOLL

DECEMBER 7

The man on top of the mountain didn't fall there.

— ANONYMOUS

DECEMBER 8

To get what we've never had, we must do what we've never done.

— ANONYMOUS

DECEMBER 9

Wisdom is knowing the right path to take...integrity is taking it.

— M.H. McKEE

Not in time, place, or circumstances, but in the person lies success.

— CHARLES B. ROUSS

Habit is stronger than reason.

— GEORGE SANTAYANA

The beginning of a habit is like an invisible thread, but every time we repeat the act we strengthen the strand, add to it another filament, until it becomes a great cable that binds us irrevocably through thought and act.

— ORRISON SWETT MARDEN

Dreams get you started; discipline keeps you going.

— JIM ROHN

DECEMBER 14

The bridges you cross before you come to
them are over rivers that aren't there.

— Gene Brown

Unless you try to do something beyond what you have already mastered, you will never grow.

— Ronald E. Osborn

In the final analysis, the one quality that all successful people have is the ability to take on responsibility.

— Michael Korda

The young do not follow our preachings – they follow us.

— Robert Brault

DECEMBER 18

Wherever you go...go there with all your heart.

— ANONYMOUS

DECEMBER 19

No person was ever honored for what he received. Honor has been the reward for what he gave.

— CALVIN COOLIDGE

DECEMBER 20

Success is the maximum utilization of the ability that you have.

— ZIG ZIGLAR

DECEMBER 21

Problems are nothing but wake-up calls for creativity.

— GERHARD GSCHWANDTNER

DECEMBER 22

Advice is like snow – the softer it falls, the longer it dwells upon, and the deeper it sinks into the mind.

— SAMUEL TAYLOR COLERIDGE

Genius is the ability to reduce the complicated to the simple.

— C. W. Ceram

People forget how fast you did a job – but they remember how well you did it.

— Howard W. Newton

We may not be able to do any great thing, but if each of us will do something, however small it may be, a good deal will be accomplished.

— D.L. MOODY

Courage is the decision to place your dreams above your fears.

— ANONYMOUS

DECEMBER 27

The end result of kindness is that it draws people to you.

— ANITA RODDICK

DECEMBER 28

A good criterion for measuring your success in life is the number of people you have made happy.

— ROBERT J. LUMSDEN

DECEMBER 29

Persistence is what makes the impossible possible, the possible likely, and the likely definite.

— ROBERT HALF

DECEMBER 30

Remember – the "free" cheese is in a mousetrap.

— ANONYMOUS

DECEMBER 31

Repetition is the mother of learning, the father of action, which makes it the architect of **accomplishment**.

— ZIG ZIGLAR

≈ *Closing Thoughts* ≈

I encourage everyone to reread books several times so that they can glean every bit of applicable information. Rereading fixes ideas in your mind that might otherwise slip away. I also suggest that my readers highlight the words that inspire, motivate, encourage and move them to new action and thought. As I've often said, when you add new information to what you already know, your creative imagination can mingle the information and present you with an entirely new perspective on the subject at hand.

I hope that over time you will find the gems of wisdom, hope and encouragement that I found when I considered what each of these quotes meant to me.

— Zig Ziglar

About the Author

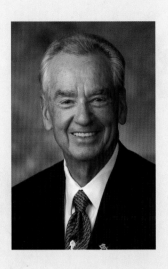

Z ig Ziglar is an internationally known speaker and the best-selling author of 27 books including the legendary classics *See You at the Top* and *Secrets of Closing the Sale*. His works have been translated into 40 different languages and dialects. He has been featured on 60 Minutes, The Today Show, and 20/20. Sixty Minutes says, **"He is a legend in the industry — the Bill Gates, Henry Ford and Thomas Edison of enthusiasm."**

From humble beginnings in Yazoo City, Mississippi, to being presented with the National Speakers Association's highest award, "The Cavett," Zig Ziglar is recognized by his peers as the quintessential motivational genius of our times. His unique delivery style and powerful messages have earned him many honors.

Today he is considered one of the most versatile authorities on the science of human potential. Having shared the stage with Presidents Ford, Reagan and Bush, Generals Norman Schwarzkopf and Secretary of State Colin Powell, Dr. Norman Vincent Peale, and Paul Harvey, Zig Ziglar is one of the most sought after personal development trainers in the world.

Titans of business, politics and sports consider him to be the single greatest influence in their lives. His client list includes thousands of businesses, Fortune 500 companies, churches, schools, U.S. government agencies and non-profit associations.

Zig Ziglar is known as possibly the greatest encourager who has ever lived. His ability to help people realize their potential is unsurpassed and his belief that, "You can have everything in life you want if you will just help enough other people get what they want," has been the foundation of all he has accomplished.

Zig Ziglar and his wife of 61 years, Jean ("the Redhead"), reside in Plano, Texas, where they attend Prestonwood Baptist Church. He is the father of four children, grandfather of seven and great-grandfather of eleven.

If you have enjoyed this book we invite you to check out our entire collection of gift books, with free inspirational movies, at **www.simpletruths.com.** You'll discover it's a great way to inspire **friends** and **family,** or to thank your best **customers** and **employees.**